BUCKBEAK

A Behind-the-Scenes Look at Everyone's Favorite Hippogriff

By Jody Revenson

A Division of Insight Editions, LP
San Rafael, California

INTRODUCTION

I n *Harry Potter and the Prisoner of Azkaban*, the first fantastic beast presented by the new Care of Magical Creatures professor for third years, Rubeus Hagrid, is a gray-and-white Hippogriff named Buckbeak. Hippogriffs are very proud creatures, Hagrid advises, and proper etiquette must be observed when meeting one (or there might be disastrous consequences). When Hagrid asks for a student to help him with the lesson, Harry Potter unknowingly volunteers when all the other members of his class back away from the offer. The professor instructs Harry to bow to the Hippogriff first, then wait to see if the creature bows back. If Buckbeak does bow, Harry can touch him. Fortunately, Buckbeak responds favorably to the salutation and not only lets Harry stroke him but also takes the student for a memorable flight. Later on, Buckbeak is very important in the rescue of Sirius Black.

"First thing you want to know about Hippogriffs is that they're very proud creatures. Very easily offended. You don't want to insult a Hippogriff. It may just be the last thing you ever do. Now—who'd like to come and say hello?"

—Rubeus Hagrid, *Harry Potter and the Prisoner of Azkaban*

A Very Mixed-Up Creature

"The Hippogriff is a kind of half-horse, half-eagle creature. Hagrid is obsessed with having pretty much lethal creatures as pets!"

—Daniel Radcliffe (Harry Potter), *Harry Potter and the Prisoner of Azkaban: Ultimate Edition*, "Creating the World of Harry Potter, Part 3: Creatures"

Hippogriffs are creatures with a long mythological history. The word *Hippogriff* comes from the Greek word *hippos*, which was their word for horse, and an Old French word, *grifo*, which came from the Latin word for griffin, *gryphus*. A Hippogriff is the offspring of a horse and a griffin, which itself is the offspring of an eagle and a lion. The designers of Buckbeak looked at legendary depictions of the creature and consulted with veterinarians so that there would be an anatomical logic to Buckbeak's shape and movement. They also visited bird sanctuaries to observe birds in flight and studied horses walking and galloping in fields outside of London.

We Can Do That!

For any film with fantasy elements, lots of discussion goes on about what will be a physical effect and what will be computer-generated. The filmmakers on the Harry Potter movies always felt it was better to have a "real" creature to interact with the actors. "In our initial meetings about Buckbeak," says creature effects supervisor Nick Dudman, "we talked about having the Hippogriff sitting down in the pumpkin patch. So I said, 'We can do that.' And they said that it would be attached to a chain, and the kids would tug on that. And I said that we could do that, too. And then they said that Buckbeak would get up and walk away with them. And I said, 'Ah, no. I don't think we can do that!'"

Horsing Around

An early idea for how to construct Buckbeak was to build it around a horse, but Nick Dudman quickly recognized the difficulty of that choice. "The way Buckbeak's head—that of a bird—was designed, you couldn't fit a horse's head into it, and how would the animal perform, anyway?" The possibility of creating just the bird front of Buckbeak in a mechanical form was suggested, but that still meant that when the entire creature was seen, it would need to be computer-generated. Eventually, it was decided that Buckbeak would be a mixture of digital and physical versions, as it was actually more economical to use full-size creatures for several scenes.

Buckbeak Times Four

"Isn't he beautiful? Say hello to Buckbeak."

—Rubeus Hagrid, *Harry Potter and the Prisoner of Azkaban*

Four variations of Buckbeak were created for *Harry Potter and the Prisoner of Azkaban* to fulfill different purposes and uses. "We had a lying-down Hippogriff that was built for the pumpkin patch," explains creature efffects supervisor Nick Dudman. "Then we had a standing Hippogriff set on a counterbalanced pole arm for foreground shots." This pole arm worked the same way a seesaw does, with a weight at the end opposite Buckbeak so that its operators could control the creature's movements. "The third was a freestanding background Hippogriff that didn't have operators attached to it, so we didn't have to use digital technology to remove them from the shot." The fourth Buckbeak was computer-generated and was used whenever Buckbeak flew or walked.

A PLAYFUL PERSONALITY

In addition to Buckbeak's physical mechanics, the animators also needed to consider what his personality would be and how it would be shown. "We did a lot of tests before we started working on the movie," says visual effects supervisor Roger Guyett. "For Buckbeak, we asked ourselves, what kind of animal is he—is he excitable? Is he sad? And how do you show that in a shot?" Early animation of Buckbeak had him jumping around in a very playful manner, acting very much like a puppy. But director Alfonso Cuarón wanted the visual effects team to "age" him up, saying that Buckbeak should be more like a "sloppy teenager." Cuarón also asked that Buckbeak be "a mixture of regal elegance when he is flying and clumsiness back on land."

A Creature of Character

"The Hippogriff scared me," says screenwriter Steve Kloves. "I mean, how are you going to bring this creature to the screen?" Director Alfonso Cuarón felt that every scene should be character-defining. "These different creatures are different extensions of the characters," says Cuarón. "The Hippogriff is one extension of Harry's coming-of-age when he discovers his inner power and his freedom." Cuarón felt that the thirteen-year-old Harry was realizing a new power he has to learn to control, and he has to learn to surrender to it in order to fly. "And once he's up in the air and extends his arms," Kloves continues, "he's no longer burdened by all the problems he has when he's on the ground. If he could only fly forever, he'd be all right."

Learning to Walk

O ne of the most important challenges in creating an original creature for the movies is to make sure they can actually do what they're supposed to do. Computers have helped this process out immeasurably. "We can understand the anatomy of a Hippogriff only up to a certain point," says creature effects supervisor Nick Dudman. "So first we create a fully realized model—a three-dimensional sculpt called a maquette—which is cyber-scanned into the computer. And, with that, the visual effects team can make the creature fly—and more important, land. Then they'll come back to us and say, 'You do realize that he'd trip over his own knees or fall to the ground when he's carrying passengers, don't you?' They'll explain that by lengthening his spine six inches, these problems would be solved." Nick appreciated these early CG studies as a very useful step in creating a realistic creature.

FIRST IMPRESSIONS

"Buckbeak was one of the most complicated elements because he was so interactive with our characters," says director Alfonso Cuarón. "That was a big challenge in terms of visual effects." The animators needed to express Buckbeak's character and his relationship to Harry Potter in the short time he is initially on screen. "Buckbeak doesn't talk," explains animation supervisor Michael Eames, "and he has a beak, with all the lack of expression implicit in that. So you look for everything that can help you convey what you want. One way was to use cues from the actors. For example, when Harry and Buckbeak first meet, we used a slight slip in Harry's posture and bounced that off Buckbeak as its reaction."

Eagle Eyes

"Now, have to let him make the first move. It's only polite. So, step up, give him a nice bow, then you wait to see if he bows back. If he does, you can go and touch him. If not . . . well, we'll get to that later."

—Rubeus Hagrid, *Harry Potter and the Prisoner of Azkaban*

Buckbeak's bird half was based on that of a golden eagle. Then visual development artists tested several color choices for his feathers, landing on combinations of gray and white. The Hippogriff's construction was supervised by key animatronic model designer Valerie "Val" Jones-Mendosa. "Buckbeak was one of the most challenging creatures I've ever worked on," she says. "We worked closely with mechanical engineers to replicate the exact wing movement and skeleton of a real bird. It took a team of twenty to build three versions of him." The animatronic model created for Harry Potter's introduction to Buckbeak could bow and move two of its legs. The Hippogriff in the pumpkin patch was able to move its wings, neck, eyes, tongue, and beak. Buckbeak's plaintive "caw" was that of a limpkin, provided by Macaulay Library at Cornell University's Lab of Ornithology.

BIRDS AND HORSES OF A FEATHER FLOCK TOGETHER

T o create the pelt on the horse end of Buckbeak, the three maquettes were "flocked." Flocking is a very labor-intensive process that involves a team of workers. First, the area to be flocked is wetted down with a special glue, and then an electrical charge is run through it. The team then fires hairs that are oppositely charged at an area. This causes the hairs to stick and stand on end. Then the hairs are combed into their desired direction before the glue dries, which has to be done within forty minutes. If this wasn't finished within the designated time period, the team would have to start again from scratch. It took a lot of rehearsing to ensure that the correct mixes of hair colors and lengths adhered to their assigned areas. Once the flocking was finished, longer hairs were punched into the models one at a time and airbrushed artwork was added.

Featherology 101

"Think he might let yeh ride him now! . . . Over here, just behind the wing joint. Don't pull out any of his feathers 'cause he won't thank yeh for that."

—Rubeus Hagrid, *Harry Potter and the Prisoner of Azkaban*

Flocking the horse half of Buckbeak was "quite a business," says creature effects supervisor Nick Dudman, "but it was nothing compared to the front half." Each version of Buckbeak required thousands of feathers to be sorted by size and then hand-dyed and airbrushed to match a specific color scheme. Chicken and goose feathers were used, though "the biggest ones at the ends of the wings needed to be fabricated" and were molded in plastic, explains Nick. Then all the feathers were glued into place one by one onto a stretchy, tailored netting that covered the models. And remember: All three Hippogriffs had to match *exactly*. Even though Nick and Val Jones-Mendosa had worked out a timeframe for the feathering, their team was still adding feathers up to the moment Buckbeak was needed on set.

Winging It

There are definite biological rules about how birds can fly that factor into their weight and wingspan. "So, obviously, to fly something the scale of a seven-foot tall horse," says visual effects supervisor Roger Guyett, "you need really big wings!" The Hippogriff's designers worked out that the wingspan length that would allow Buckbeak to fly would be twenty-eight feet. Except that wings that size would drag on the ground when he walked and possibly even trip the Hippogriff. So, "essentially we cheated," confesses visual effects supervisor Tim Burke. "We had smaller wings when he was on the ground and bigger wings when he was flying. But hopefully you won't notice."

Featherology 102

Buckbeak's animators had as formidable a task as the creature effects team when it came to feathering the creature. As the Hippogriff is seen in full daylight and close up, the feathers needed to be as realistic as digitally possible, something that up to this point had been a challenge to computer artists. In order to achieve this, the team created the individual types of feathers to as fine a detail as possible and then designed a computer program that would move the feathers together in the same way as a real bird's. Additionally, Buckbeak's wings needed to go from wrapped against his body to extended while flying and vice versa. "We had to develop a wing that could move from fully outstretched to fully folded without interruption," says CG supervisor David Lomax. "The grooming and packing of the feathers had to be precisely correct." And they needed to achieve all this without revealing that Buckbeak had different wing lengths to perform these two actions.

Year of the Hippogriff

I took about a year to create Buckbeak, from drawing the initial concepts to filming the Hippogriff's scenes with Daniel Radcliffe, Robbie Coltrane, and the other actors. Creature effects supervisor Nick Dudman recalls that the design phase began in June 2002. "You have a period of time where you conceptualize the creature," says Nick, "for which the art department produced many preliminary drawings. That's narrowed down, and then you progress to the maquettes, which you can show the filmmakers. They can walk around it and ask questions about its size and movements." Maquettes of the Hippogriff were created in November, and final approvals came in January. "The creature went on set in May 2003, so you're looking at nearly a year of involvement," Nick explains. The digital decisions and creation of Buckbeak happened simultaneously, but the manufacturing period of the physical creature took four and a half months of solid work.

Beak on a Stick

In addition to the three life-size models, various other filming techniques were used during the interactions between Buckbeak and the actors. When Harry Potter (Daniel Radcliffe) is allowed to stroke the Hippogriff after their bows to each other, and, after he returns from their flight, he was actually stroking a beak on the end of a stick! This ensured that when Daniel touched the beak, we would see the correct curvature of his hand for the action. Stroking something in empty air would not have given it this realism. The beak puppet was removed digitally, and the full CGI Buckbeak was then added in.

DOING WHAT COMES NATURALLY

"Come on, Buckbeak ... Come and get the nice dead ferret..."

—Hermione Granger, *Harry Potter and the Prisoner of Azkaban*

The filmmakers went to great lengths to ensure that Buckbeak was as realistic as a fantastical creature could be. "It's so realistic," director Alfonso Cuarón says, "that if people watch carefully, in the scene where Buckbeak is in the paddock, you will see he actually poos. Buckbeak poos!" Cuarón came up with the idea when the team was observing the movement of horses for reference: "I saw that the horses would be very casually, very naturally, pooing. So it's not a big deal; it's just a matter-of-fact thing that Buckbeak does."

A LIGHT HORSE

There were several occasions when a real horse would stand in for Buckbeak during rehearsals so that the visual effects crew could observe how the light through the trees would shade the creature and how the shadow of the creature itself would be cast on the environment. This lighting was re-created exactly in the computer. The digital team looked for all ways possible to lend authenticity to their creations, which constantly impressed the filmmakers. "When you see Buckbeak in the movie," says executive producer Mark Radcliffe (no relation to Daniel), "and he's placed in the live-action scene, matching the light of the set with how the light falls onto the Hippogriff and the shadow movement in relation to the other actors—it is seamless."

Taking Flight

Once Harry and Buckbeak are introduced, Hagrid places the student on his back for a test flight. Daniel Radcliffe (Harry Potter) shot the sequence in a blue-screened room in a way similar to filming broom flight. But instead of hanging from wires, Daniel sat on a full-size model of just the Hippogriff's trunk that was attached to a rig arm, which was also covered in blue-screen material. The rig would reproduce preprogrammed movements provided by the animation team and was filmed by a camera that was also synced to the action. Visual effects then "composited" a filmed background of the Hogwarts grounds, the CG Hippogriff, and the footage of Daniel to create a seamless scene. They even added clouds of digital dirt that fall from Buckbeak's hooves when he takes off and lands!

On Location

The "sitting-down" version of Buckbeak in Hagrid's pumpkin patch was constructed in England and brought to Glencoe, Scotland. Typically, an operator would be placed in a close proximity, but the Hippogriff would be sitting atop a granite hillside, so creature effects supervisor Nick Dudman knew it couldn't be operated from underneath: "We could radio-control it, but then you have to deal with great thumping motors. Where do they go? How do we deal with the sound?" Nick decided to use a variation of hydraulics called *aquatronics* for Buckbeak's big movements. This system uses cables pumped through with water instead of the oil used in hydraulics and creates smoother, more graceful shifts that can give the creature more elegance and gravity. The crew needed to be graceful, too, and not tread on the cables and damage them. Any noticeable cables were digitally erased in postproduction.

IT NEVER RAINS, BUT IT POURS!

Buckbeak was placed in the Scottish hillside location by means of a crane, "which was a ghastly experience," creature effects supervisor Nick Dudman recalls. "This was done during the middle of a soaking rainstorm. The muddy hillside's being washed off, then replaced with more mud, and it's all rolling down!" Nick was concerned about rain getting into the creature's electronics. "It's not something you can service easily," he continues. "You can't run off to the nearest shop and buy a new part! And while filming, we had to stop every two minutes because of downpours of rain or hail and throw tarpaulins over it to protect it, while all the time we're sliding about in the mud. It certainly wasn't the way to treat a complex animatronic creature!" But Nick admits, "We got some great footage, so, you know, in the end, it was all worth it."

Biting Hot

"You're not dangerous at all, are you, you great ugly brute."

—Draco Malfoy, *Harry Potter and the Prisoner of Azkaban*

A ctor Tom Felton, who played Draco Malfoy, remembers his scenes with Buckbeak, which were shot in Black Park, about an hour west of London. "I remember it very clearly," he says with a laugh, "because it was very sunny and very hot that day. We did the first shots with our black robes on over our clothes, but that changed immediately! It was so bloody hot, you'll notice that all the top buttons on our shirts are undone." Many of the students were also allowed to take their robes off. Draco fails to follow Hagrid's advice and storms up to Buckbeak without the proper etiquette, only to get struck down. "Hagrid picks me up, but in order for that to work size-wise, they had to make a very realistic one-third size life cast of me," Tom says. "I asked if I could take it home. I thought it was a brilliant thing; I could have put it in my bed, like I was sleeping, and go out!"

Make It Your Own

One of the great things about IncrediBuilds models is that each one is completely customizable. The untreated natural wood can be decorated with paints, pencils, pens, beads, sequins—the list goes on and on!

When making a replica, it's always good to study an actual image of what you are trying to copy. Look closely at the images in this book and brainstorm how you can re-create them.

Before you start building and decorating your model, though, read through the included instruction sheet so you understand how all the pieces come together. Then, choose a theme and make a plan. Do you want to make an exact replica of Buckbeak or something completely different? The choice is yours! Here is an example to get those creative juices flowing.

WHAT YOU NEED

- Black, white, gray, golden yellow, and red paint
- Paintbrush

WHAT YOU MIGHT WANT

- Gouache (used in example)

GOUACHE PAINT is a type of opaque watercolor that blends very nicely. You can find it at your local arts and crafts store. If you don't have gouache, acrylic paint will work, too.

PAINTING BUCKBEAK

1. Assemble the model, but leave the wings off.

2. Start by painting the midsection of the model white. This includes Buckbeak's front legs, chest, and stomach.

3. Paint Buckbeak's back legs, tail, and head gray.

4. Add an extra coat of gray to the beak.

5. Paint the ends of the front legs gray.

6. Since Buckbeak's feathers are speckled, go over the white midsection with small dabs of gray paint. Blend them in with the white background until you achieve the effect you like.

7. Now, go over the gray back legs, tail, and head with white paint. Add small dabs of paint, and blend them in until you are happy with the effect.

8. Finish with the small details: white hooves, black claws, and golden eyes.

PAINTING THE WINGS

1. On the engraved side, paint the top section of feathers white. Speckle them with gray just as you did on Buckbeak's body.

2. Paint the rest of the feathers gray.

3. Using a small paintbrush, carefully paint stripes onto each feather with a lighter shade of gray.

4. For the unengraved side of the wings, paint the top of each wing white.

5. Paint the rest of the wing gray, and add speckles of white over it.

6. Finish by adding a section of vertical black markings down the middle of the wings where the white meets the gray.

IncrediBuilds™
A Division of Insight Editions, LP
PO Box 3088
San Rafael, CA 94912
www.insighteditions.com

 Find us on Facebook: www.facebook.com/InsightEditions
Follow us on Twitter: @insighteditions

 Copyright © 2016 Warner Bros Entertainment Inc. HARRY POTTER characters, names and related indicia are © & ™ Warner Bros. Entertainment Inc. WB SHIELD: TM & © Warner Bros. Entertainment Inc. J.K. ROWLING'S WIZARDING WORLD ™ J.K. Rowling and Warner Bros. Entertainment Inc. Publishing Rights © JKR. (s16)

Library of Congress Cataloging-in-Publication Data available.

ISBN:978-1-68298-021-7

Publisher: Raoul Goff
Art Director: Chrissy Kwasnik
Designers: Jenelle Wagner and Ashley Quackenbush
Executive Editor: Vanessa Lopez
Managing Editor: Molly Glover
Associate Editor: Greg Solano
Production Editor: Elaine Ou
Editorial Assistant: Warren Buchanan
Production Manager: Thomas Chung
Production Coordinator: Sam Taylor
Model Designer: Ryan Zhang, Team Green

Buckbeak visual development artwork by Dermot Power, Paul Catling, and Andrew Williamson.

INSIGHT EDITIONS would like to thank Victoria Selover, Melanie Swartz, Elaine Piechowski, Ashley Bol, Margo Guffin, George Valdiviez, and Kevin Morris.

Insight Editions, in association with Roots of Peace, will plant two trees for each tree used in the manufacturing of this book. Roots of Peace is an internationally renowned humanitarian organization dedicated to eradicating land mines worldwide and converting war-torn lands into productive farms and wildlife habitats. Roots of Peace will plant two million fruit and nut trees in Afghanistan and provide farmers there with the skills and support necessary for sustainable land use.

Manufactured in Shaoguan, China, by Insight Editions

10 9 8 7 6 5 4 3 2